Two Weeks, Twice a Year

two weeks, twice a year

COLIN THOMAS

Two Weeks, Twice A Year
first published 1994 by
Scirocco Drama
An imprint of J. Gordon Shillingford Publishing Ltd.
© Copyright Colin Thomas, 1988

Cover design by Terry Gallagher/Doowah Design
Author photo by Lincoln Clarkes
Printed and bound in Canada by Hignell Printing Ltd.

Published with the generous assistance of The Canada Council.

Canadian Cataloguing in Publication Data

Thomas, Colin, 1952-
Two Weeks, twice a year

A play.
"Scirocco Drama"
ISBN 0-9697261-5-5

1. Title
PS8589.H4575T86 1994 C812',54   C94-910750-6
PR9199.3.T56T86 1994

J. Gordon Shillingford Publishing
4252 Commerce Circle, Victoria, BC V8Z 4M2

Production Credits

Two Weeks, Twice a Year was originally commissioned and produced
by Green Thumb Theatre for Young People and premiered on January
21, 1988, at the Maplewood Community School, North Vancouver,
B.C., Canada, with the following cast:

JOE...................................Jacques Lalonde
GOGO...................................Scott Bellis
MOM...................................Maribel Tait
DAD................................Brent Applegath

Directed by Kathryn Shaw
Designed by Ken MacDonald
Stage Manager: Syvia Swift
Dennis Foon was the artistic director of Green Thumb Theatre.

Acknowledgements

Heartfelt thanks to the kids and parents who shared their stories with me in dozens of interviews.

Thanks as well to everyone who worked so hard to make the first production a success, and to the Canada Council for their support.

Scene List

My Room

(The main room in the set is a kid's bedroom. There's one single bed and a huge collection of toys and junk. JOE comes running in and GOGO is just behind him, cheeks puffed out and apparently full of water.)

JOE: No spitting! No spitting, Gogo. That's gross! It's disgusting!

(GOGO advances on JOE. JOE grabs GOGO's teddy-bear, Boinkley.)

You spit on me, Gogo, and I throw Boinkley right out the window. I swear. And some dog'll rip his head off.

(GOGO indicates that he wants his teddy.)

Swallow first.

(GOGO makes an elaborate show of swallowing the water, and his cheeks deflate, but he holds his head back as he speaks.)

GOGO: Okay.

(GOGO grabs the teddy...and then spits the water, which he has been saving in his mouth, at JOE.)

JOE: You pig!

(JOE grabs a pillow off the bed and swings it. GOGO grabs a pillow, too, and they both go at it. GOGO is getting the worst of it. Then he lunges at JOE and the two of them are wrestling. They fall all over the room, trashing it in the process.)

No biting. No biting, Gogo. That's for wimps. You're not a wimp, are you?

(And the fight's back on. At one point, JOE rips the covers off the bed and throws them over GOGO's head. He wraps his arms around GOGO's waist.)

You give? You give?

GOGO: No!

(JOE wrestles GOGO, who's still inside the blankets, so that he has GOGO in a headlock. JOE rubs his knuckles over the blanket on GOGO's head.)

JOE: Goobers!

GOGO: I give! I give!

(They both laugh, exhausted. JOE suddenly notices the audience. He points them out to GOGO. Then they get up and address the audience directly.)

JOE: Hi. My name's Joseph Andrew McAlpen O'Rourke and I'm twelve. But everybody calls me Joe.

GOGO: And my name's Joseph Andrew McAlpen O'Rourke too, but my mom and dad and everybody calls me Gogo, because when I was a baby I couldn't say Joseph, so I just said Gogo and that's what they called me.

JOE: We're the same guy, except that I'm twelve.

GOGO: Yeah, and I'm six, but we're the same guy.

JOE: In this play, we tell you stuff that's happening now, when I'm twelve, and I play those parts.

GOGO: And we tell you stuff that happened a long time ago, when I was six, and I play those parts.

JOE: And this is my room. *(To GOGO.)* Boy, we trashed this place! It looks like a bomb exploded. *(Throws the bedclothes in the air, to be a bomb.)* Bcchh!!

GOGO: *(To JOE.)* Yeah, so let's clean it up now, okay, please?
             Mom said you had to do it today, before Dad gets here.

             (To the audience.) Our mom and dad are divorced and our
             dad's coming for a visit today...

             *(JOE takes the contents of the garbage can and throws
             it into the air.)*

JOE: Uh-oh. here come more bombs. Bcchh!! Bcchh!!

GOGO: *(To JOE.)* Joey! What if Dad comes in here and it's all
             messy and he goes, "Oh! Do pigs live here or something?"

JOE: Okay, okay already. If we clean up, will you shut up?

GOGO: Okay.

JOE: Ho-ly! We got about two minutes before Mom gets home.
             Emergency clean-up.

             *(JOE starts racing around, clearing away the mess
             and making siren noises. GOGO soon catches on.
             GOGO grabs the garbage can and JOE tries to shoot
             stuff into it like he's shooting baskets. This is fine until
             JOE is about to throw Boinkley into the trash.)*

GOGO: No!

JOE: Why not?

GOGO: He's mine.

JOE: What? You think he's got feelings? We gotta throw out
             some of your baby stuff.

GOGO: No way.

JOE: Well, we've gotta throw something out.

             (GOGO grabs JOE's guitar.)

GOGO: Okay. How 'bout your guitar?

JOE: No way! Dad gave me that.

GOGO: So what? You still can't play it.

                   *(They look at one another then count to three as they
                   very cautiously exchange the guitar and Boinkley.)*

JOE /GOGO: One. Two. Three.

JOE: I make up new songs on it and everything.

GOGO: Sure, sure.

                   *(Goaded into it, JOE plays two lines of his new song
                   loud and fast.)*

JOE: *Rita, Rita, you look so cool.*
                   Rita, Rita, I feel like a fool...

                   I made that up.

                   *(GOGO sticks his fingers down his throat and pretends
                   to gag.)*

                   Who cares what you think? I'm gonna play it for Dad when
                   he gets here. He says I could be a professional musician.

                   *(Falling into a fantasy of being a rock star, JOE
                   assumes a rock star pose. GOGO makes fun of him.)*

                   What are you staring at? I thought you wanted to clean up.

                   *(GOGO starts the siren sound and for a couple of
                   moments both boys throw things under the bed and
                   into the closet. GOGO finds a photograph that's been
                   hidden away.)*

GOGO: Hey! Is this Rita from the song?

JOE: Gimme that! No! It's nobody!

                   *(JOE lunges for the picture, but GOGO won't let him
                   have it.)*

GOGO: So why do you have her picture then? It is! She's your
                   girlfriend!

(GOGO turns around and twines his arms around himself, doing the classic smooch and feel-up gag.)

Oh, Rita, Rita, Rita! I love you so much! Oh, Rita, I want to kiss you!

(JOE grabs RITA's picture out of his hand and shoves him away.)

JOE: Turkey.

(GOGO tries to get another look at the picture. JOE hides it from him.)

GOGO: You can have it. I don't care.

(The boys sit on the bed and look at the picture.)

You like her, eh? Girls! Ecchhh!

JOE: You'll understand when you're older.

GOGO: Yeah. But when I get older, I turn into *you*.

Laundry

(MOM enters the house, dressed in her bus driver's uniform.)

MOM: Joe? Joe, I'm home!

GOGO: It's Mom! Oh, no! We better clean up.

JOE: Chill out. Just stash some stuff under the blankets.

(GOGO and JOE start cleaning up the room. GOGO is frantic. JOE is trying to stay cool. Downstairs, MOM changes from her work jacket and shoes to her sweater and slippers.)

MOM: What are you doing up there?

JOE: Um…cleaning up my room.

MOM: Well, good!

JOE: Yeah! I'm almost finished.

(GOGO doesn't know what to do with the garbage can.)

Don't worry about that. Just stash it.

(The garbage can goes under the covers with everything else.)

Now stay out of this! She can't see you, remember? This is my part of the story.

GOGO: But we're not finished yet.

JOE: Stay out of it!

(GOGO hides somewhere—maybe under the bed. He will emerge later to observe the scene—possibly perched on a window ledge.

JOE does some last minute tidying and finishes with a spectacular leap across the bed just as MOM enters his room.)

MOM: Well!

(MOM looks around.)

Well…it's a start anyway. Good for you.

(MOM goes to put an arm around JOE and give him a kiss, but he squirms out of her embrace.)

JOE: Mom!

(MOM notices the pile on the bed.)

MOM: What's under the covers?

JOE: Laundry. I thought I'd do it myself.

MOM: That's okay. I was just going to throw some stuff in the washer.

(MOM makes a move to pick it up.)

JOE: No, no. You relax. I'll do it.

(MOM backs off, confused.)

MOM: O-kay.

(MOM sits down on the bed, right next to the lump, which makes JOE very nervous. She notices the picture of RITA.)

Hey, who's this?

JOE: Mom! Nobody. Look. Oh, geez…forget about it. Forget you even saw it there.

MOM: Oh, relax already.

JOE: Mom! Just give it here.

MOM: I think she's pretty. Listen, if you ever have any questions about girls, or dating…

JOE: Yeah, yeah, yeah, yeah, yeah.

MOM: Well, I know about dating. And I used to be a girl.

            (JOE tries to ignore her.)

            And I know how embarrassing it is when you think somebody's cute.

JOE: Mom! Leave me some pride.

MOM: All right. All right. Forget it. I'll just take this downstairs.

            (MOM starts to pick up the laundry to carry it downstairs.)

GOGO: Uh oh!

MOM: Hey! What's in here?

JOE: Laundry?

            (MOM throws the cover off JOE's pile of stuff.)

MOM: Geez, Joe, I thought you cleaned up!

JOE: Yeah, well. I was just starting…

MOM: How long did this take you, five minutes?

JOE: I'll clean up tomorrow.

MOM: Sure, right in the middle of your dad's visit. All right, that's it. No more TV—and that includes video—till you get this place together.

JOE: Mom!

MOM: I am not your maid.

            (JOE kicks the bed in frustration.)

You got something to say about it?

JOE: Why? Why should I have to clean up my room just because you think it's dirty? You've got the whole rest of the house to play with. This is *my* room.

MOM: Then *you* clean it.

JOE: I already do more housework than any other kid I know. I do your stupid dishes.

MOM: My stupid dishes! What do you eat off, the floor?

JOE: I probably could. I vacuum your stupid rug. Every week!

MOM: Oh, cry me a river!

JOE: I'm telling Dad.

MOM: What? That I force you to scrape your underwear off the floor every six months?

JOE: Maybe I should just go live with him.

MOM: Don't *give* me that! Just...don't give me that.

JOE: No, but really. Really. I mean it. Maybe I should just ask him.

MOM: No. Read my lips because I'm not going to tell you this again. No. And I don't appreciate it when you use your father as blackmail.

JOE: But what if he said I could?

(MOM sighs. She's heard all this before.)

MOM: Look, I know you're all wound up 'cause your dad's coming and everything. But I don't want this whole weekend to turn into a hassle. You know what I'm saying? Stop asking me if you can live with your father, okay?

JOE: I'm a boy.

MOM: So?

JOE: So maybe boys should live with their fathers.

                  *(MOM puts one hand on top of JOE's head and clamps
                  the other under his jaw, shutting him up.)*

MOM: Stow it.

                  (Beat.)

                  And if you don't clean up your room, I'm gonna do it. And
                  then I get to decide what gets thrown out.

                  *(MOM exits. JOE grabs his guitar. He beats out some
                  chords and starts to sing.)*

JOE: *I hate my mother 'cause she's such a drag!*
                  I hate my mother 'cause she's such a nag!
                  I hate my mother 'cause she's such a...bag!!

Don't Go

GOGO: You told her you wanted to move to Toronto.

JOE: So?

GOGO: So what about me?

JOE: So come if you want.

GOGO: No way! I like it here.

JOE: No kidding! Why don't you just stay here and be mommy's little suckybaby? I'll go to Toronto.

GOGO: No!

JOE: You're both so boring. You and Mom.

GOGO: No way! You can't leave me here, anyway. You can't! We're always together.

JOE: Maybe I could. Maybe I could just leave you in this room all by yourself and nobody'd ever come to visit you. Not even Mom.

GOGO: No, Joe, don't go away. Don't leave me, okay? I won't bug you anymore, I promise. Just don't go away and leave me, okay?

JOE: Okay, okay.

GOGO: Promise!

JOE: Okay, I said. Don't worry about it. You're probably right. I couldn't leave you, even if I tried.

(JOE puts his hand on GOGO's shoulder.)

Don't cry about it or nothing. Now, go play somewhere else, okay? It's almost time for Dad to come.

GOGO: Do you think he can see me?

JOE: No.

GOGO: You sure?

(JOE nods his head.)

Okay.

(GOGO looks around for a place to hide and chooses the closet.)

Waiting

(JOE spins around and turns on his tape deck. He dances wildly before he turns the tape deck down and speaks.)

JOE: It's hard to know what to wear, eh? I don't want to get all dressed up and look like an idiot, but I don't want to look like too much of a scuzzbag, either.

(GOGO throws the closet door open to offer JOE some alternatives. JOE rejects a couple of shirts, then finds one that he likes. It's the same sweatshirt that DAD gives JOE in the scene called 'Sweaters.')

So I put on my best sweatshirt and I gel my hair up and everything. Like, when he gets here, I usually feel like hugging him and punching him right in the head all at the same time. And I usually feel like puking, too. Wouldn't that be cute? Open the door—"Hi, Dad,"- baaarrff! Like, all over his good suit. There's nothing to do, so I go to the living-room to cool out.

(JOE takes the tape deck downstairs, turns it up, and dances in the living-room. MOM enters, all dressed up. She turns the tape deck down and fixes her hair.)

But of course he's late and my mom's watching every second tick by like it's another point against him. Tick, tick, tick—two thousand points! He's not your father anymore.

(JOE turns the tape deck back up and dances wildly. MOM turns it off.)

MOM: Can you do me up?

JOE: Where you going?

MOM: Out with the girls.

            (JOE pinches MOM with her zipper as he tries to do her up.)

MOM: Ow!

JOE: Sorry.

MOM: Relax, why don't you? He'll get here.

            (MOM does herself up.)

JOE: Mom? Do I look stupid, or am I the perfect pre-teen?

MOM: Perfect pre-teen.

            (The doorbell rings. JOE manically checks himself out at the mirror before summoning all his cool.)

MOM: Why don't you just open the door?

JOE: I'll get it. I'll get it. Just stay cool.

            (JOE practices answering the door before he opens it.)

            Hi, Dad!! No, no. Hi, Dad. All right. Hi, Da…

            (JOE opens the door. He is mid-greeting when a huge, inflated Godzilla roars into the room.)

Godzilla

(DAD is roaring behind Godzilla. MOM screams.)

DAD: It's Godzilla, the lizard that ate Vancouver.

MOM: Geez, Mark!

(DAD roars behind Godzilla.)

Can't you just walk in a door?

DAD: No, as a matter of fact. Not without bringing something for my favourite boy. So, whaddya think?

JOE: Oh, yeah, he's cool. Where'd you get him?

DAD: One of those stores on the way over. I was drivin' past and I saw him in the window. So, you like him or what?

JOE: Oh yeah, he's awesome, man. Truly magnificent.

DAD: Awesome? I think I scored.

So, how ya doin', Gogo? Long time no see.

JOE: Good.

MOM: Nobody calls him Gogo anymore, Mark.

JOE: Dad can if he wants.

DAD: Thanks.

(There's a long pause. All three are awkward.)

DAD: How's tricks, Sal?

MOM: *(Too quickly.)* Excellent. Couldn't be better.

(Another pause. They're at a loss for words.)

MOM: Joe, why don't you give your dad a hug?

JOE: Mom!

DAD: Sounds okay to me.

              (DAD opens his arms for JOE to come for a hug. His attitude is one of fooling around, but when JOE falls into his dad's arms, they both hug hard and they mean it. MOM is smiling from ear to ear.)

              Something funny?

MOM: No, no. It's just really good to see you guys—you know—expressing your feelings like that.

DAD: Oh. Yeah. You're just on your way out, are you?

MOM: Why do I feel like I'm getting kicked out of my own house?

DAD: Hey, Sal, it happens to the best of us.

MOM: You're not going to keep him out too late, are you?

DAD: No, no. Not too late. Just late enough.

MOM: I love it when you come to visit. It makes me so sure divorce was the right decision.

              (To JOE, as she's heading to the door.) Don't stay out all night, eh? Have fun!

JOE: 'Bye.

DAD: 'Bye.

              (MOM exits. DAD and JOE look at one another and howl like wolves.)

              So let's introduce Godzilla to your room.

JOE: Then let's go, 'kay?

              (JOE grabs Godzilla, and JOE and DAD step into

JOE's room. GOGO is sitting on the bed, holding Boinkley.)

DAD: Holy smokes!

JOE: What?

DAD: Nothing's changed in here. It's all just the same as when you were little. Hey, here's whatsisname...

(DAD picks Boinkley out of GOGO's lap.)

JOE: Boinkley.

DAD: Right.

JOE: *(Grabbing Boinkley and hiding him away somewhere.)* I keep trying to put him away. He just...gets back out!

(DAD finds JOE's chest expander.)

DAD: Hey, you into body-building?

JOE: Yeah.

DAD: So, you think you can take me?

JOE: I doubt it.

DAD: Come on.

JOE: I seriously doubt it. Besides, we'd probably wreck stuff.

DAD: *(Looking around the room.)* In here? What's the matter? Chicken?

JOE: No.

DAD: So come on. Just thumb-wrestling, like when you were little. Come on!

(JOE grabs DAD's hand in the thumb-wrestling grip. GOGO gets right into this, too, although he obviously can't have contact with DAD. He stands upstage and enthusiastically goes through the motions. He quietly shares the opening lines.)

DAD/ JOE/GOGO:

> One! Two! Three! Four! Let's have a thumb war! Shake.
> Bow. Begin!

> *(DAD and JOE start to thumb-wrestle. It gets pretty
> wild pretty fast.)*

JOE:

> No fair! You're moving your arm!

DAD:

> There are no rules in love and thumb-wrestling.

JOE:

> All right!

> *(JOE whips DAD's arm around so that it's behind his
> back. DAD throws JOE onto the bed and tickles him.
> JOE's laughing and screaming. He loves it. They're
> wrestling flat out.)*

DAD:

> You give?

JOE:

> No!

> *(DAD rubs his knuckles on JOE's head. JOE laughs
> and screams some more.)*

DAD:

> Goobers! You give?

JOE:

> Yeah, yeah. I give.

DAD:

> I didn't hear you!

JOE:

> I give! I give!

> *(DAD releases JOE. They're both panting and
> laughing.)*

DAD:

> You can almost take me, you know.

> *(JOE tackles DAD again, trying to tickle him.)*

> No, come on. Cut it out now. Cut it out.

JOE:

> Why?

DAD:

> 'Cause I gotta get my stuff down to the hotel and take you
> out to dinner. Okay? Let's go.

(DAD takes a last look at the room before they exit.)

Think we wrecked anything in here?

JOE: Naa, just rearranged it.

DAD: Yeah.

(They exit, punching.)

Berlin Wall

(GOGO releases Boinkley from his hiding place, then wanders around the room, being a bored little prisoner, till he picks up JOE's guitar. He can't play or sing, but he hits the strings and hollers.)

GOGO: *Oh, Rita, you are my girlfriend.*
Oh, Rita, I love you so mu-u-u-uch.
Oh, I just love girls and I want to get married!

(GOGO throws the guitar on the bed.)

He thinks he's so smart. 'Suckybaby!'

(GOGO addresses Godzilla as if the monster were JOE.)

Hey, Joe! Yeah, you're just about as ugly as him, too. Think you're pretty smart, don't ya?

(GOGO smacks Godzilla and makes the monster roar in response. He improvises a fight with the monster. Godzilla roars "Suckybaby!" GOGO rides the monster like a pony, bodyslams him, and is eventually the victor. JOE comes barging in the living-room door and yells upstairs to GOGO.)

JOE: Gogo! Hey, Go!

(GOGO stops playing immediately. He becomes cool and restrained. He's still casual when JOE enters the bedroom.)

Oh man, it was so cool! I decided for sure I'm gonna ask him.

GOGO: What?!

JOE: No, listen. I was with Dad for four and a half hours. He let me eat anything I want, even the stuff Mom says is going to give me cancer. And then we went to *Karate Kid–Part Forty-Five* or something. It was so cool. And at the end there's this fantastic fight, and he still does this one, you know?

(JOE does the famous kick, balanced on one foot.)

I love that. It's so cool. So, when I see him tomorrow…I'm gonna ask him if we can go live with him in Toronto.

GOGO: No! I don't have to go to Toronto if I don't want and you can't make me.

(JOE pauses, then changes gears completely.)

JOE: Hey, have you been fooling around with my stuff?

GOGO: Didn't touch it.

JOE: Oh yeah? Then why's my guitar on the bed and what's Godzilla doing in the middle of the floor?

GOGO: Didn't touch it.

(JOE starts throwing his stuff and GOGO's stuff into two separate piles.)

JOE: You know what I think? I think we should divide the room in half. You get half and I get half.

(JOE throws Boinkley.)

And you can keep all your baby stuff on your side. And I'll keep all my junk on my side. And if you even think about even breathing on my junk, I'll punch your lights out.

(JOE moves his guitar and Godzilla onto his side of the room.)

And, in case you have any trouble remembering that this is my side of the room, let's say there's a line right down the middle, and there's barbed wire on it, all right?

> *(JOE pinches along the line till he gets to GOGO, then he pinches him.)*

All right? That's what barbed wire feels like.

GOGO: Ow! Cut it out! Cut it out!

JOE: And let's pretend there's a great big saw blade that comes along the border and it chops your feet off if they're sticking across. You better watch out, 'cause here it comes. Chop! Chop! Chop!

GOGO: Joey, stop it.

JOE: Chop! Chop! Chop!

> *(JOE hits GOGO on the leg, hard, with the heel of his hand.)*

GOGO: Ow! That hurt. *(Crying.)* You pig!

JOE: Well, you should stay on your side of the line.

GOGO: I am! I am on my side of the line.

> *(Beat.)*

What'd I do? I didn't do anything.

> *(Beat.)*

JOE: It was just so—cool!—with him. And I want to go live with him. But you won't let me.

> *(Beat.)*

Why not, Gogo?

GOGO: Because he's mean, like you.

JOE: He is not.

GOGO: Is too. Don't you remember when they used to fight?

JOE: That wasn't his fault.

GOGO: Mom cried!

JOE: You used to like him. He called you his favourite boy.

GOGO: They used to fight.

Fight

(DAD and MOM can be heard offstage. They are mid-fight.)

MOM: Talk to me! I just want to talk.

DAD: Forget it. I can't talk to anybody who's screeching at that decibel level.

MOM: I am not screeching. I'm just trying to make myself heard.

GOGO: Remember?

JOE: Yeah.

(DAD and MOM enter the living-room.)

MOM: We *have* to talk about this.

DAD: There's nothing to talk about.

MOM: You quit another job! What am I supposed to do, start moonlighting?

(In the bedroom, GOGO hugs Boinkley and starts to quietly chant "Shut up." JOE closes his eyes and mouths the chant along with GOGO.)

DAD: Just don't be a martyr, all right? I'm not falling for it.

MOM: Mark, there's not enough money. What about food? We have a child, for God's sake.

DAD: Don't get hysterical. Nobody's starving.

MOM: Mark!

DAD: What do you want me to do? Take some crummy job for the rest of my life? Well, forget it! I'm a musician.

MOM: You're not a musician if nobody's paying you for it. Music is your hobby.

DAD: Just back off, all right? Music is not my hobby!

MOM: Well, it's not paying the rent. It's time to start acting like a grown-up. I can't support all of us.

DAD: So whaddyou want? You want me out of here, is that it? Because if that's what you want, I'm outta here. I'm gone!

MOM: Just forget about the music and get a real job.

DAD: No! I can't do that!

MOM: Well, if that's your bottom line, why don't you just get out of here, then? Get out!

        (Finally, the boys can't stand it anymore. They leap to their feet and shout.)

GOGO/JOE: Shut up! Shut up! Shut up!

        (MOM and DAD stop fighting. They look towards the bedroom, then awkwardly, guiltily, at one another.)

MOM: Goey?

Sweaters

GOGO: Stay out of this. This is my part of the story.

JOE: What?

GOGO: Don't you remember what happens next?

JOE: Yeah, they come in here and talk to me.

GOGO: No. They come in here and talk to *me*. They can't see you now. I'm six.

(JOE hides himself, maybe behind Godzilla. MOM and DAD enter the bedroom.)

MOM: Gogo? Honey? Are you all right?

(To DAD.) Now look what we've done.

Gogo?

(MOM goes over and pats the lump of blankets that is GOGO.)

MOM: It's okay. We're not fighting anymore.

(GOGO rolls over and looks at his mom. He doesn't see his dad.)

GOGO: Is Daddy going away?

(Beat.)

Where's he going to go to?

DAD: I'm not going anywhere right now. Want me to stay with you while you fall asleep?

(GOGO looks at his mom, then his dad.)

Let's let Mommy go to sleep, okay? I kinda want to talk to you by myself.

GOGO: No. I want you both to stay.

DAD: *(To MOM, dismissing her.)* It's okay. I think we're all right in here.

MOM: Mark, he wants us both to stay. We should probably talk about this…together.

DAD: We do a real good job of talking to one another, don't we?

       (Beat.)

This is going to be hard enough. Let me talk to him alone, please. Please.

MOM: Goey?

       (MOM takes off her sweater and hands it to GOGO.)

Here, you wrap this around Boinkley. It'll help him go to sleep. I'm just gonna go downstairs for a minute.

GOGO: No.

MOM: Yeah. It'll be all right. I'll just be downstairs.

       (She hugs GOGO and gives him a pat on the head.)

We'll talk tomorrow, okay honey? Okay.

       (MOM exits.)

GOGO: When you yell, Boinkley can't get to sleep, you know.

DAD: *(Picking up the bear.)* Sorry, Boinkley.

Goey? I'm gonna go away for a little while, but I'm always gonna be able to see you, okay?

GOGO: *(In a small voice.)* No.

DAD: Sorry, Go. I have to.

GOGO: Why?

DAD: Because Mommy and I fight all the time.

GOGO: Well, then I wanna come with you, then.

DAD: But then who's gonna take care of Mommy? She can't be here all by herself.

              (GOGO doesn't answer.)

              I won't go far away. And you know what? I'll give you my phone number so you can phone me up whenever you want.

GOGO: *(Starting to cry.)* I don't want to talk to you on the telephone. I hate the telephone. I don't know why you can't just stay here.

DAD: Well then, you're just gonna have to visit all the time. And then maybe when you get big, you can come and live with me. All right? When you're bigger, you can live at my house.

              (Beat.)

              It's gonna be okay. Just wait. Hey, just a minute.

              (DAD takes off his sweatshirt and hands it to GOGO.)

              You wrap this around Boinkley, too. You can keep that if you want.

              (Ruffling GOGO's hair.) Hey. Who's my favourite boy?

GOGO: I am.

              (DAD goes to exit, then he turns.)

DAD: You got any questions?

GOGO: Dad?

DAD: What?

GOGO: *(Near tears.)* I dunno.

DAD: I know what you mean.

            (It's too painful for DAD to embrace GOGO, so he exits. GOGO buries his face in Boinkley again. JOE speaks to GOGO.)

JOE: But that was the night he promised, eh? He promised we could go and live with him when we got older. Remember?

GOGO: Yeah, but he promised he'd come visit, too...

JOE: He came.

GOGO: ...and he never.

JOE: He came all the time at first.

GOGO: At first, but then hardly ever. And then he moved to Toronto.

JOE: Your fault.

GOGO: Was not! What'd I do? What'd I do? I didn't make him move to Toronto.

JOE: Yes! Remember that time he came to visit and he brought that present?

            You didn't have to be so mean.

GOGO: I didn't do anything. I was not mean. I wasn't.

JOE: When he got here, he was all in a good mood and everything. He was trying to be nice. Remember?

Transformer

(DAD enters through the living-room door, carrying a large gift-wrapped present.)

DAD: Gogo! Go?

JOE: *(In the bedroom, to GOGO.)* He had it all wrapped up and everything.

DAD: Hey, Go-bot, where are ya? I've got something for ya.

(JOE urges GOGO to go out the bedroom door and talk to DAD.)

JOE: Go on.

(GOGO steps into the living-room. DAD howls in greeting. GOGO responds with a mini howl.)

DAD: What are you standing there for? Don't you want to see your present?

GOGO: What's it for? It's not my birthday or anything.

DAD: I just saw it on the way over. I thought you'd like it.

(GOGO meticulously starts taking off the wrapping. He will take forever doing this.)

How's your mom doin'?

GOGO: Okay.

DAD: She ever ask about me?

(GOGO doesn't respond.)

How about you? *(Beat.)* What's the matter? Don't feel like talking?

GOGO: You can talk if you want.

(GOGO finishes unwrapping the present. He holds it up.)

DAD: Optimus Prime. You still like him on cartoons?

(GOGO starts to play with the Transformer as deliberately as he unwrapped it. DAD gets up and moves around.)

Um, I've got something else to tell you, actually. I'm not going to be able to pick you up next week.

(There is the slightest pause in GOGO's activity.)

I got a gig in Winnipeg, so I gotta go there for a couple o' weeks.

(Pause.)

But this job won't last so long. So not next week, but the week after, okay?

GOGO: I don't care. You can go wherever you want to.

DAD: *(Indicating the Transformer.)* That a tricky one?

GOGO: Easy. A baby could do it.

DAD: Maybe I should just take it back, then.

GOGO: I'll keep it.

DAD: Okay. Look, I don't have time to hang around right now, okay? But I'll talk to you before I go.

(Beat.)

Hey, who's my favourite boy?

(DAD goes to ruffle GOGO's hair, but GOGO shifts out of the way.)

GOGO: Mom cries, you know.

             (Beat.)

             You should know. You made her do it.

DAD: I know you're mad at me, but it's not just my fault.

GOGO: *(Shoving his gift back at DAD.)* It's so easy. A baby could do this.

DAD: I'll see you in a couple o' weeks, okay?

             (GOGO returns to the bedroom. DAD takes the wrapping, but leaves the Transformer somewhere that GOGO can get it, then DAD exits.)

Molson's Clock

JOE: And then, a little bit later, he moved to Toronto.
Why didn't you just tell him you never wanted to see him
again?

GOGO: It wasn't my fault.

JOE: Well whose fault was it then?

GOGO: His.

JOE: Oh, yeah. For sure.

GOGO: He doesn't even love us. Remember that time when he just
took off? He didn't even say goodbye or anything.

JOE: I don't wanna hear this again, all right?

(GOGO throws on a windbreaker.)

GOGO: Yes. Before he went to Toronto, he was supposed to come
for a goodbye visit and he was going to pick me up at two
o'clock. So I went outside to wait on the porch and it was
raining, but I wanted to see him the minute he got there.

*(GOGO grabs the Transformer and runs downstage.
He's on the porch.)*

JOE: And then the phone rang.

(MOM comes out to GOGO.)

MOM: You better come back inside, honey. Your dad's not gonna
make it today.

GOGO: No way! Who says?

MOM:	Your dad says. When he called he was at the airport. He's on his way to Toronto.
GOGO:	Liar.
MOM:	Gogo...
GOGO:	Liar!
MOM:	He said they need him for work right away and he had to fly out.

(GOGO doesn't respond. He starts to hum The Beatles' 'Yellow Submarine'.)

MOM: Gogo. One thing about your dad. Sometimes...he doesn't like to say goodbye. He doesn't like people to see him cry.

(Beat.)

Come on, let's go inside.

GOGO: I wanna stay here.

MOM: It's okay to feel sad.

(Beat.)

We could put on some music.

GOGO: I like it out here.

MOM: Honey...okay.

(MOM goes back into the house.)

GOGO: I waited. And waited. Because I didn't believe her. I waited on the step for three hours. And the Molson's clock? You know that big clock on the beer building. I watched every minute. And every minute I would say, "I know he's coming, because he loves me. I know he's coming because he loves me." But he didn't. And at six o'clock, I gave up.

(Short pause.)

It was cold out there in the rain. I could've got ammonia.

JOE: You could've got what?

GOGO: Ammonia.

JOE: You mean pneumonia.

GOGO: Same difference.

> *(JOE has gotten up and gotten his guitar. He starts to play and sing.)*

JOE: *In the town where I was born*
lived a man who sailed to sea...

GOGO: What are you playing that for?

JOE: Remember when he used to sing that to us?

GOGO: Yeah. Before we went to bed. I used to hold the guitar and he would do the fingers and sing.

JOE: Let's you and me do it.

GOGO: No. I did that with Daddy.

JOE: Come on. I can do the fingers. I can. Come on. Let's try it.

> *(JOE places his guitar on GOGO's lap and wraps his arms around him to hold the guitar.)*

You do the strings.

GOGO: I know. I know that already.

JOE: Okay.

> *(GOGO strums as JOE does the fingering for the chords.)*

GOGO/JOE: *(Singing.) In the town where I was born*
lived a man who sailed to sea
and he told us of his life
in the land of submarines...

JOE: Gogo, if you believed he loved us, would you go to Toronto?

GOGO: Yes.

JOE: Okay. It's a deal.

(GOGO throws his windbreaker into the closet and lies down on the bed as JOE gets up to address the audience.)

Room Service

JOE: Tonight I get to go to my dad's hotel. It's our last night, so I get to stay really late.

            (DAD enters the hotel room, playing his guitar. If that guitar is electric, it will be referred to as a Fender Jaguar; if acoustic, as a Gibson J200. JOE enters, sneaks up behind DAD, and howls like a wolf. Startled, DAD laughs, then he howls too. DAD holds out his guitar to show JOE.)

            Can I see it?

DAD: Sure.

            (DAD hands JOE his guitar and JOE examines it.)

JOE: Fender Jaguar!

            (DAD nods. JOE's impressed.)

            So I guess work's goin' good, huh—your band and everything?

DAD: Oh, man! Yeah. I finally—finally!—feel like I'm makin' it. The band is *this* close! We got an album coming out this summer and if this one makes it big—that's it, your dad's a rock star.

            (JOE strikes a rock star pose with the guitar.)

JOE: Rock and roll!

DAD: Only trouble is, I don't get half enough time to see you.

JOE: Yeah. Prob'ly be better if I lived there. Or, like, if we lived closer anyway.

DAD: So are you just gonna sit there huggin' that thing, or are you gonna play it? How 'bout some of your own tunes?

JOE: Na-a-aw.

DAD: Come on. You wanna be a professional musician, you gotta play in front of people.

JOE: None of 'em are any good!

(DAD gives JOE his guitar pick.)

DAD: Play.

(JOE plays and sings.)

JOE: *Rita, Rita, you look so cool.*
Rita, Rita, I feel like a fool.
I like your looks,
Let me carry your books.
If you walk away from me…

(DAD hesitates.)

See what I mean?

DAD: No, wait a minute, wait a minute.

(DAD takes the guitar and quietly works on the song.)

It's a love-song, right?

(JOE goes all goopy.)

JOE: Dad!

DAD: If it's a love-song, why don't you sing it like this?

(DAD sings the same lyrics, to a new, improvised arrangement. DAD has a little trouble remembering the words, so JOE feeds them to him. They sing the final line together.)

JOE: Yeah. That's cool.

DAD: Well, it's a cool song.

(Beat.)

So this Rita...you like her?

JOE: Yeah.

DAD: That's cool too.

   (DAD howls. JOE howls. They both laugh.)

JOE: Yeah, and she's cute, too!

DAD: How cute?

JOE: Mega-cute!

   (They both howl and laugh.)

DAD: You guys go out?

JOE: No way! I never even talk to her.

   (DAD's putting his guitar away.)

DAD: Well...there's no big rush. *(Beat.)* Is there?

JOE: No. Dad! What are you talkin' about? You're as bad as Mom.

DAD: So how *are* things with your mom, anyway?

JOE: Okay.

   (Beat.)

Dad?

DAD: What?

JOE: She bugs me!

DAD: Unh huh.

JOE: She's a non-stop bug machine.

DAD: Unh huh.

JOE: Seriously. Like she's always bugging me about my room
              and everything. And she's gotta know all about my private
              life.

DAD: She likes to be close.

JOE: Close! Yeah, but...she's sitting on my head!
              I don't even know why I have to live with her anymore.

              (In the bedroom, GOGO sits up and watches them.)

DAD: Because she has custody.

JOE: But, if she said, then I could come live with you, right?

DAD: Let's not talk about things that aren't gonna happen, all
              right? But you know I'd like to. 'Cause you know I love ya.

JOE: *(To GOGO.)* He loves us, Goey. I'm going to ask him.

GOGO: What about Mom?

              *(DAD howls, then starts to contort and shudder. It's as
              if he's turning into a werewolf.)*

JOE: *(To DAD.)* What's the matter? What's happening?

DAD: *(Attacking JOE.)* Wolves need...meat! *(Suddenly normal.)*
              You wanna go get a pizza?

JOE: *(Laughing.)* Yeah, sure.

              (DAD and JOE fool around as they leave the room.)

GOGO: Joey! What about Mom?

              (JOE stops and looks at GOGO.)

DAD: Come on. Let's go.

              (JOE turns away and exits with DAD.)

Together, Forever, Whatever

GOGO: He better ask her! When Dad left, she took care of me.

MOM: *(Entering the living-room.)* Damn!

(MOM is carrying two pieces of broken vase. She sucks a small cut on her finger, then her hand starts to shake and she cries. She sits on the sofa.)

GOGO: She cried all the time at first. It was scary, but I helped her.

(GOGO comes down from upstairs, carrying Boinkley.)

MOM: *(Noticing him.)* I'm sorry, Gogo. This is stupid. I'm just like a water fountain. *(Beat.)* I know you miss him. But I miss him, too.

GOGO: *(As if Boinkley is saying it.)* Don't worry. I'll be your friend.

MOM: Aw, thanks, Go.

(Beat.)

Goey, I want you to know that I'll never leave you, all right? No matter what happens, I will never leave you.

GOGO: I won't leave you either.

MOM: I guess we're pretty lucky, actually. Because we've still got each other. Forever.

GOGO: Yeah.

MOM: Together forever.

GOGO: Whatever happens. Forever.

MOM: Hey! "Together, Forever, Whatever." Hey, we're poets and we didn't even know it.

              (MOM starts to laugh.)

              Not bad! I didn't even mean to do that. Did you?

GOGO: No.

MOM: *(Seriously.)* I don't know what I'd do without you, Goey. I don't.

              (Beat.)

              And I have the perfect excuse to throw out that stupid vase. I never liked it anyway...

              (GOGO runs and picks up a garbage can. MOM drops the broken vase into it.)

              It was a wedding present.

              (GOGO exits. JOE starts calling from outside the door as MOM enters JOE's room and picks up Boinkley. JOE enters by the living-room door.)

Asking Mom

JOE: Mom! Mom!

MOM: In here.

JOE: Where?

MOM: Your room.

JOE: What are you doing in there? You're not messing up my junk are you?

MOM: Relax.

JOE: It's my stuff, so just don't touch it, all right? It's private, so just leave it, okay?

(JOE barges into the bedroom. MOM is sitting on the bed, holding Boinkley. She hasn't touched another thing.)

What are you doing?

MOM: Thinking.

(Beat.)

About your bum.

JOE: What?

MOM: You had the cutest little bum when you were a baby. You were so fat!

JOE: Mom!

MOM: And when I used to change your diapers, you know what I'd do?

JOE: No, what? I'm dying to know. Please tell me. Please.

MOM: When I'd cleaned you up and I'd wiped all the muck out of the creases in your fat little legs, and got you all washed and powdered, I'd lean over and kiss you right on your butt.

JOE: Mom!

MOM: It was irresistible. Like a magnet.

JOE: Oh, thank you very much! Mom, that is so gross! What are you telling me that for?

MOM: Because there's something about having a baby that makes you feel...I dunno...

              (GOGO enters the playing area behind MOM and JOE and watches them. He's like a ghost.)

              There's this little human being and it's yours and it's perfect. And you want it to stay perfect and you don't want anything bad to ever happen to it. You know what I'm saying?

JOE: Sort of. But I'm not a baby anymore. *(Beat.)* Actually, I've got something pretty important to ask you.

MOM: You want to go and live with your dad.

JOE: How'd you know...?

MOM: Lucky guess.

              (Beat.)

              Ask him. I hope he says 'yes.'

JOE: What? Oh, geez! Thanks!

MOM: *(Half-joking.)* Just don't forget your poor old mom, eh?

              (JOE doesn't know what to say. He hugs MOM.)

JOE: Are you kidding? But will you be all right...with the housework and everything?

(MOM laughs.)

MOM: I think I'll manage, yeah. *(Beat.)* Hey, maybe now I'll be the one who gets to fly in and buy you presents and everything.

JOE: Yeah.

MOM: When are you going to ask him?

JOE: Tomorrow morning. Before his plane leaves.

MOM: And if he says 'yes', when do you want to go?

(JOE shrugs.)

Just don't be in too much of a hurry, okay?

(JOE nods and MOM exits. JOE addresses the audience directly.)

JOE: All of a sudden, I start cleaning my room for the first time in, like, years!

Asking Dad

JOE: And in the morning, I go down to my dad's hotel.

            (JOE exits by the living-room door.

            In the bedroom, GOGO puts on his windbreaker, and grabs Boinkley and his suitcase. He sits on the suitcase and waits, eager to observe the scene below. He looks just like he did six years earlier when DAD left for the first time.

            DAD is in his hotel room, packing. JOE walks right in. JOE howls to get DAD's attention.)

DAD: Hey! What's up? I thought we said goodbye last night.

JOE: Yeah, but...

DAD: What?

JOE: Well, I got a new sleeping bag, you know.

DAD: What?

JOE: Well, if I bring it to Toronto, you won't have to get new sheets or anything...

DAD: What are you talking about?

JOE: Mom said I can come live with you if you want!

DAD: What? No she didn't.

JOE: *(Excited, very quickly.)* Yes she did! Isn't that fantastic? I never thought she would, but...probably the best time for me is the Easter break, if that's okay with you. Then I can start my new school after the break. And I won't bug you about your work, or anything. But, if I stay out of the way, I can probably come with you on a couple of your gigs, right?

DAD: Wait a minute. What is this? I'm not involved, so nobody talks to me?

JOE: Well, yeah , but…you said you wanted to. Last night.

DAD: Of course I want to, but…

JOE: But what?

DAD: But what I *want* doesn't have anything to do with it. I mean, I work every night. I'm never home.

JOE: Yeah, but that's okay. I can take care of myself. Or, like, I could stay with somebody else…

DAD: Joe, there's just no way.

JOE: *(Keeping up his enthusiasm and pressure to the last minute.)* …or you could have somebody check up on me or something. Why not?

DAD: No. It's just not going to work. You should've talked to me about this.

            (JOE looks at DAD, stunned, shaking his head.)

            What?

JOE: You're unbelievable.

DAD: It's not that bad. It's not like we're never going to see one another again. Look…

            (DAD makes a concilliatory move towards JOE, but JOE stands up to avoid him. In the bedroom, GOGO stands up at the same time.)

JOE: Forget it. I don't even want to see you anymore.

DAD: Hey! You don't mean that.

JOE: Yes, I do. I don't even want to see you.

(JOE starts to bolt for the door. DAD tries to stop him.)

DAD: Joe...

JOE: Get your hands off me.

(JOE runs out of the hotel room. GOGO returns his suitcase to the closet. DAD checks his plane ticket then runs after JOE.

JOE re-enters through the living-room door and returns to the bedroom. He speaks to GOGO.)

JOE: So I guess you can relax. We're not going to Toronto.

(JOE punches the bed. Carrying Boinkley, GOGO sidles up to him and tries to put a hand on his shoulder.)

GOGO: It's all right. We'll still be okay here with Mom.

(JOE grabs Boinkley and hurls him across the room.)

JOE: Just shut up, you stupid baby. Just get out of here.

(Terrified, GOGO retreats to the wall, just beside the closet door. JOE curls up in a foetal position on the bed.)

Guitar

(MOM and DAD enter JOE's bedroom.)

MOM: Joe, your dad's here.

JOE: So what?

DAD: I want to talk to you.

JOE: Too bad.

              (MOM and DAD look at one another.)

MOM: Come on, Joe. He missed the plane so he could come back here.

DAD: Come on. Talk to me.

              (DAD touches JOE's shoulder, but JOE pulls away. JOE sits up on the bed and is very cool. JOE looks at MOM and she indicates that JOE should talk to DAD.)

JOE: So, if you've got something to say, why don't you say it?

              (DAD nods at MOM and she exits.)

DAD: I know you're mad at me and everything because you can't come to Toronto. But it's crazy there. I'm never home. But that doesn't mean you're gonna stay mad at me forever, does it? We can still visit.

              (GOGO stands up. He's directly behind DAD and JOE.)

JOE: You said that when I was six.

DAD: When I lived here, we used to visit all the time.

GOGO: All the time at first...

JOE: All the time at first, and then hardly ever.

DAD: You wanna know why? You wanna know what it was like going back to my apartment after seeing you and your mom? Like having my heart cut out with a dull knife. I've never been so lonely in my life.

          (JOE drops his head.)

GOGO: I've been lonely. Ever since you left.

DAD: That's why I moved. Because I love you so much I couldn't stand not being with you all the time. I thought maybe a clean break...

JOE: Oh, sure. You left because you just loved me so much.

DAD: Remember what it was like before I moved? Every time I saw you we'd fight and cry...

          (JOE's frustration with this is physical. GOGO's is audible.)

GOGO: *(To DAD.)* It wasn't my fault!

          (DAD can't hear him. GOGO looks at JOE.)

DAD: I just felt useless. You and your mom...

GOGO: It wasn't my fault! *(To JOE.)* You tell him.

DAD: You didn't make it much easier, either. You were always on her side, you know.

JOE: *(Finally breaking.)* What was I supposed to do? I was just a little kid.

          (Pause.)

DAD: *(Finding it hard.)* I'm sorry. Joe, I can't tell you...

JOE: *(Interrupting.)* Sorry what? Sorry you left? Why'd you do it, then?

(DAD makes a move to touch JOE. JOE moves away.)

DAD: Joe...

GOGO: Joe, listen.

JOE: Why'd you do it?

            (Pause.)

DAD: I had to. I had to work. When I went to Toronto, it was like...I got work and it was like it saved my life. I might've been a failure as a husband and a father, but at least I could play, you know what I mean?

            I know I can't make it up to you, but...but I was thinking. Maybe you could come out for a month this summer. Or maybe for the whole summer if we can swing it...I figure I can afford to hire somebody for a couple of months. You know, for night-times when I'm away.

            (JOE doesn't respond.)

            Come on. Gimme a break here, Joe. I'm trying.

JOE: I don't wanna come for the stupid summer. You promised when I got bigger, I could come and live with you. You promised!

DAD: Joe, I never...

JOE: You did! And now I can't even come and live with you. You're just trying to buy me off! I don't wanna spend the summer with some stupid babysitter!

DAD: Well, maybe you'd like me to quit my job, then, but I can't do that.

JOE: Then why don't you just get out of here, then?

DAD: Because we need each other, Joe. I'm your father.

JOE: No, we don't. I don't even need you. I don't even have a dad.

(Pause. DAD gets up and moves slowly to the door. He turns around.)

GOGO: Joe. He's crying.

DAD: What you said is not true. I will always be your dad. And I will always love you.

(DAD goes down to the living-room to talk to MOM.)

GOGO: He does. He loves us, Joey.

(Downstairs.)

DAD: Well, that was brilliant.

MOM: Give him time.

DAD: You tell him I'll be waiting.

(Upstairs.)

GOGO: Joe! He's leaving.

JOE: So what?

GOGO: He loves us.

JOE: He left.

GOGO: He's our only dad.

He said he's sorry. He said so.

(Downstairs, DAD is getting his stuff together and heading for the door. He and MOM might even have a final hug. GOGO is frantic.)

What if he leaves this time and we can't get him back, ever, ever, ever?

JOE: Who needs him?

GOGO: I do.

(Beat.)

I do.

(JOE doesn't respond. In a desperate attempt, GOGO calls DAD from the top of the stairs.)

Dad! Daddy!

He can't hear me, Joe. Don't let him leave, Joe. Not again.

If you let him leave this time, it really will be your fault.

JOE: *(Lurching to his feet. Calling.)* Dad! Dad?

DAD: Yeah?

(DAD comes running into JOE's room, followed by MOM.)

Yeah, what?

JOE: Dad? Um...

(JOE clears his throat.)

You know that new arrangement you did on my song? I can't quite get it the way you did it.

DAD: Oh, well...you want me to show you?

JOE: Yeah, if you've got a minute. I don't want you to miss another plane or nothing.

DAD: Forget about the plane! There's nothing I'd rather do. Joe, um...

(DAD's trying to thank JOE, but he can't find the words.)

...can I use my old guitar?

JOE: Sure.

(DAD picks up JOE's guitar. He looks at MOM, who smiles and exits.

JOE notices GOGO, who's dying to get in on this.)

             Dad? You remember when I was just a little kid and you used to sing *Yellow Submarine*?

DAD: Yeah.

JOE: Do you think we could do that?

DAD: Really? You wanna do that instead?

             (JOE gets up to lure GOGO towards DAD, who can't see them.)

JOE: Yeah. Just pretend I'm little.

             (JOE speaks to GOGO.)

             Come on.

             (GOGO shakes his head 'No.')

             Come on.

             (JOE insists and drags GOGO forward.)

             I used to love it.

             (JOE pushes GOGO forward. DAD looks up and sees GOGO. Beat. A huge smile lights up DAD's face and GOGO smiles back. They're really seeing one another.)

DAD: All right then. Let's do it.

             (GOGO snuggles in front of DAD, with the guitar on his lap. DAD puts his arms around GOGO to play the chords. It's a hug.)

             All right! Oh, God, I loved doing this, too. It was the best, eh?

GOGO/JOE: Yeah.

DAD: You just strum and I'll do the chords.

GOGO/JOE: I know. I know that.

DAD: Okay, here we go. Ready?

(GOGO nods. All three of them sing and play.)

DAD/GOGO/JOE:

> *In the town where I was born*
> *Lived a man who sailed to sea*
> *And he told us of his life*
> *In the land of submarines.*
>
> *We all live in a yellow submarine,*
> *Yellow submarine, Yellow submarine.*
> *We all live in a yellow submarine.*
> *A Yellow submarine, Yellow submarine.*

DAD: Hey, who's my favourite boy?

GOGO/JOE: I am.

> *(They hold the tableau, then the cast takes the curtain call together.*
>
> *The End.)*

Due